LIFE INSIDE THE
COAST GUARD
ACADEMY

AILEEN WEINTRAUB

HIGH
interest
books

Children's Press®
A Division of Scholastic Inc.
New York/Toronto/London/Auckland/Sydney
Mexico City/New Delhi/Hong Kong
Danbury, Connecticut

Book Design: Daniel Hosek
Contributing Editor: Eric Fein

Special thanks to Jim Dempsey

Photo credits: Cover, pp. 7, 9, 13, 16, 19, 21, 23, 25, 26, 29, 31, 33, 34, 39 courtesy of
United States Coast Guard; pp. 20, 22 courtesy of Defense Visual Information Center,
March ARB, California; pp. 5, 37, 41 © Reuters NewMedia Inc./Corbis; p. 10 © AFP/
Corbis; p. 15 © James A. Sugar/Corbis

Library of Congress Cataloging-in-Publication Data

Weintraub, Aileen, 1973-
Life inside the Coast Guard Academy / by Aileen Weintraub.
    p. cm. -- (Insider's look)
Includes index.
Summary: Explores the challenges and rewards of attending the United
States Coast Guard Academy in New London, Connecticut, where individuals
are trained to become Coast Guard officers.
ISBN 0-516-23925-2 (lib. bdg.) -- ISBN 0-516-24002-1 (pbk.)

1. United States Coast Guard Academy--Juvenile literature. [1. United
States Coast Guard Academy. 2. Occupations.] I. Title. II. Series.
V437 .W45 2002
363.28'6'07117465--dc21

                                                                    2002001903

CONTENTS

Introduction

"I do solemnly swear that I will support and defend the constitution of the United States against all enemies, foreign and domestic, and that I will bear true faith and allegiance to the same, and that I take this obligation freely. . . "

The preceding pledge is part of the oath taken by cadets of the United States Coast Guard Academy. Taking the oath is the first step toward a challenging career in the U.S. Coast Guard. The Coast Guard Academy's purpose is to train men and women to be officers in the U.S. Coast Guard. Cadets who enter the U.S. Coast Guard Academy are signing up to save lives. The academy molds and shapes young men and women into the leaders of tomorrow. These leaders serve their communities and country in many ways.

A college education is very important in today's society. People who want more than a traditional college experience may be interested in attending the Coast Guard Academy. This military academy provides men and women with a first-rate, free education. It also offers a rewarding career and unlimited adventures.

Have you ever wondered what life is like at the U.S. Coast Guard Academy? Or what it takes to get in? This book will give you an insider's look into this unique school. You'll learn that life in this academy can be exciting and very busy. Let's take a closer look at life in the U.S. Coast Guard Academy.

Graduates of the Coast Guard Academy are trained to be ready for action. They are dedicated to protecting their country whenever called upon.

CHAPTER ONE

History in the Making

When the U.S. Coast Guard Academy first started in 1876, all classes took place on board a sailing ship. The academy was originally called the School of Instruction for the Revenue Marine. The school trained nine cadets aboard a schooner called the *Dobbin*. A schooner is a type of ship with two or more masts. The *Dobbin* worked out of Fisher Island near New Bedford, Massachusetts. In 1878, a new ship, called the *Chase*, replaced the *Dobbin*. The *Chase* was a barque, which is a ship with three or more masts. The *Chase* remained in Arundel Cove, Maryland.

In 1900, shoreside classes were added to the shipboard training programs. Over the years, the academy moved to two other ships called cutters: the *Itasca* and then the *Hamilton*. In 1914, the name of the academy was changed to the Revenue Cutter School of Instruction.

In 1932, the academy moved to its present location on the Thames River in New London, Connecticut. The 126-acre campus has twenty-six buildings. However, cadets still train on sailing ships. The academy's barque, the *Eagle*, sails all over the world while cadets train on board.

The Coast Guard Academy campus has the latest high-tech equipment and labs to teach its cadets.

SHIPS AHOY!

The *Eagle* is the largest of the United States' tall ships. It is also the only square-rigger in U.S. government service. This "classroom on the sea" is 295 feet long. It holds twelve officers, thirty-eight crewmembers, and an average of 150 cadets. The ship itself has an interesting history. The *Eagle* was acquired from Germany after World War II (1939–1945). It was taken as a U.S. war prize. It was built in Hamburg, Germany, in 1936, where the German navy used it as a training ship. Four other ships that look exactly like the *Eagle* were also built in Germany. Together, these ships were called the "Five Sisters." Early in World War II, the *Eagle* became a cargo ship, but was still used in training missions.

After the war, with the help of the German crew on board, the *Eagle* sailed from Bremerhaven, Germany, to its new homeport in New London, Connecticut. The *Eagle* is where Coast Guard Academy cadets get their first taste of life at sea. This is also where they put into practice the navigation and engineering skills they've learned in the classroom.

A whole lot of sailing going on! The Coast Guard
Academy's barque, the *Eagle*, has 21,350 sqaure

COAST GUARD ACADEMY BASICS

"Belief in your country. Belief in your fellow cadets and Coast Guard personnel. And belief in yourself." This motto sums up the Coast Guard Academy's philosophy, or main ideas. The Coast Guard is considered a humanitarian force. This means that it was created to

Oil and water don't mix! Academy cadets are trained to handle slippery situations like this oil spill.

help others. Helping others could mean being part of a search-and-rescue team. It could mean working to save the environment from oil spills or stopping illegal drug traffic. Although the Coast Guard's main mission is to help save lives, Coast Guard members are also trained and ready for combat if the need arises.

The Coast Guard Academy is also an engineering school. The academy is the smallest of the five military academies in the United States. After four years of hard work at the academy, a cadet receives a bachelor of science degree and a commission as an ensign in the U.S. Coast Guard.

Going to the academy means accepting certain limitations. For the first two years at the school, cadets must wear a uniform within 50 miles of the academy at all times. There's no sleeping late or missing class at this school. Public displays of affection, including hand-holding, are also out of the question.

The Coast Guard Academy requires cadets to balance a rigid academic schedule with mandatory athletic requirements. It also requires that they learn to follow strict military codes.

CHAPTER TWO

Getting In and Staying In

Like every college, there are requirements to meet in order to be accepted. The Coast Guard Academy expects you to have good grades and be between the ages of seventeen and twenty-two. You must be unmarried and physically fit. You must also be a U.S. citizen.

Unlike other military academies, the Coast Guard Academy does not require a recommendation from a U.S. senator or congressperson. The cadets are admitted to the academy based solely on merit. Cadet hopefuls must pass a detailed physical exam. They must also score high on the Scholastic Aptitude Test (SAT) or the American College Testing Assessment (ACT). The only high school test scores that will be accepted are the ones for tests taken

March on to greatness! The Coast Guard Academy teaches its cadets to stand tall under any circumstances.

through December of your senior high school year. High school class rank is also very important.

The Cadet Candidate Evaluation Board looks over an applicant's total file and history. Then the board makes their decisions based on your overall accomplishment during your high school years. They want to see motivated leaders. This can be demonstrated by a student's participation in extracurricular activities, community involvement, and any part-time jobs. Recommendations from teachers, coaches, and other mentors are also taken into consideration.

Individual reasons for wanting to attend the academy are also very important. Applicants should have a strong desire to serve their nation and to help save lives.

Tuition to the academy is free and there is no application fee. If accepted, however, cadets must pay a one-time fee of $3,000. Cadets get a monthly salary that covers expenses like books, uniforms, and personal items.

Each year, the Coast Guard Academy accepts about 275 new applicants. Approximately 850 cadets are enrolled at the academy every year. Attending requires a solid commitment and four years of hard work. After the four years, cadets must then serve in the U.S. Coast Guard for five years.

Play the field! In addition to an applicant's
record, the Coast Guard Academy loo[ks]
each applicant spends his or her time in e[ach]
activities, such as sports.

In 1976, the Coast Guard Academy became the first f the four armed-services academies to admit man cadets.

WOMEN IN THE ACADEMY

In the past, the military has been a man's world. That has been true of the military academies as well. However, times have changed. More and more women are entering the armed services. Approximately 30 percent of cadets at the Coast Guard Academy are women. The requirements for men and women are the same. However, physical standards are adjusted according to gender. For example, women and men do the same types of pull-ups, but a different amount. To cadets, gender doesn't make a difference. Once cadets enter the academy, their goals are the same: to graduate and become a Coast Guard officer. They're all in it together.

SWAB SUMMER

Swab Summer is a freshman cadet's first experience in the Coast Guard Academy. All new cadets are called fourth class, or swabs. Swab means "mop" in coast guard slang. Cadets quickly get used to the special words that are used in the Coast Guard. For example, the stairs are called ladders, the floor is the deck, and the beds are racks.

Swab Summer is like no civilian college experience. It starts in July and lasts seven weeks. Cadet's must give up many of the comforts they enjoyed in the past. Watching television at any time and staying out late is not allowed. Cadets must also memorize many military codes and rules. The swabs go through intense physical training. They quickly learn how important teamwork and friendship are during this time.

A FOURTH CLASS CITIZEN

During their first year, cadets have fewer rights and less liberty, or leave time, than other cadets at the academy. All cadets live in Chase Hall. Living quarters at the academy are called barracks. As part of their training, fourth class cadets must run in the middle of the barracks hall, arms pressed to the sides of their bodies and bent at right angles. They must keep their heads and eyes straight forward. If their eyes stray, an upper classman can give them demerits. Demerits are bad marks on a person's academic records, which may lead to extra weekend duty or restriction of privileges.

THIRD CLASS

Life gets a little easier during the cadets' second year at the academy, but not by much. Academically, cadets have a heavy course load, as they will the entire time they attend the academy. During the summer before second year, cadets sail aboard the training ship the *Eagle* for five weeks. They spend three weeks at a coast guard unit and two weeks sailing small boats.

Cadets are put through tough physical training to prepare them for life in the Coast Guard.

ACADEMY FACTS

If an upper classman asks a swab the question: How long have you been in the Coast Guard mister? The swab must reply, "All me bloomin' life. Me father was King Neptune, me mother was a mermaid. I was born on the crest of a wave and rocked in the cradle of the deep. Me eyes is stars, me teeth is spars, me hair is kelp and seaweed, and when I spits, I spit tar. I tough I is, I am, I are."

SECOND CLASS

Second class cadets are those in their third year at the academy. They take on added responsibilities, such as training fourth class cadets. They tell the swabs what to do, when to do it, and how to do it. The second class's summer program involves a lot of training, too. This is the year they sharpen their leadership skills. They get specialized shipboard training instruction as well as rifle, pistol, and aviation training.

Upperclassmen cadets keep the swabs in line.

FIRST CLASS

First class cadets have the most privileges. They get to sleep the latest, have the most leave time, and can even have a car on campus. It is their job to supervise the second class cadets. During the summer before senior year, the first class spends ten weeks aboard a Coast Guard cutter. This is where they learn and practice their responsibilities as junior officers in the military.

ACADEMY FACTS

Cadets at the academy have uniforms for every occasion. These uniforms must be kept neat at all times. This means ironing them every day and polishing the uniform's buttons and buckles. Cadets must also shine their shoes until they can see their own reflections in them.

During the summer between their first and second years at the academy, cadets get their sea legs during daily training on the academy's barque, the *Eagle*. The trip on the *Eagle* lasts five weeks.

CHAPTER THREE

Day to Day at the Coast Guard Academy

At the academy, morning starts at 6:00 A.M. for third, second, and first classes. That is when reveille sounds. Reveille is a wake-up call played on a bugle. However, swabs get up at 5:30 A.M. to deliver papers, empty the trash, and clean the bathrooms.

Breakfast ends by 6:45 A.M. Then it's off to military training. Cadets put in 16-hour days with hardly any free time. Classes start at 8:00 A.M. and go until 3:00 P.M. After that, cadets concentrate on athletics.

The average upper classman has about eighteen class hours per week. If cadets have free time, they most likely spend it studying. This may seem like a rigid schedule, but it is nothing compared to a typical day on board a

The only way to succeed at the academy is by working hard. Cadets put in long hours of study—in and out of class—each day.

U.S. COAST GUARD ACADEMY MAJORS

- Civil Engineering
- Electrical Engineering
- Mechanical Engineering
- Naval Architecture and Marine Engineering
- Operations Research
- Marine and Environmental Sciences
- Management
- Government

Coast Guard officers and civilians work as classroom professors and teachers at the academy. Cadets get a first-class education under their instructors' watchful eyes.

cutter on long patrol. The academy's goal is to prepare cadets for the realities of shipboard life.

THE CLASSES

Classes at the academy are designed to prepare cadets for life in the Coast Guard. Unlike other military academies, the Coast Guard Academy has both officers and civilians as professors. The core classes that every cadet must take include chemistry and physics, math, government, and humanities. Most of the majors involve engineering. Literature, writing, and history classes are also taught at the academy.

A Coast Guard officer must be organized and a good leader. To help cadets learn these skills, the academy gives classes in leadership and organizational development. These are classes that may not be found at civilian colleges. There is also a strong academic support system for the cadets at the academy. If a cadet is struggling with his or her studies, there is a lot of help available.

THE HONOR CONCEPT

WHO LIVES HERE REVERES HONOR, HONOR'S DUTY. These words appear in large brass letters on the floor of Chase Hall. Lying, cheating, or stealing are not tolerated at the academy—under any circumstances.

At the academy, living with honor is a way of life. Cadets must be able to trust each other here as they will serving in the Coast Guard. Therefore, breaking the honor code is taken very seriously and called a Class 1 offense. Anyone who breaks the honor code can get kicked out of the academy.

Skipping class, being disrespectful to upperclassmen, or coming back late from liberty, a day off, are all grounds for punishment. As punishment, a cadet may have to work additional hours or participate in extra marching tours. Liberty may also be taken away.

A Ship-Shape Room

Everything in a cadet's room, such as clothing, must be kept in a specific location. The number of personal items that a cadet may display is limited. For example, he or she can only have a certain number of photos on the shelf in his or her room. This rule is strictly enforced. Inspections are common at the academy. Upperclassmen put on white gloves and check for dust and dirt in a cadet's room. Personal appearance is also very important. If a cadet's clothes are wrinkled or his or her shoes are scuffed, that cadet could be given demerits. After all, these cadets will be representing the nation as Coast Guard officers.

From the moment they arrive, cadets are taught to live and work following the academy's honor code.

Sports and Leisure

Athletics are a very important part of life at the Coast Guard Academy. Sports help to develop character, encourage teamwork, courage, and self-confidence. Cadets must take part in either varsity intercollegiate teams or in intramural programs. They may also participate in club sports. Football, track, wrestling, sailing, fencing, and lacrosse are just some of the sports available to cadets.

Each cadet must also become an excellent swimmer. Cadets are constantly tested on their fitness levels and swimming skills. If they don't make the grade, they are given help. If they still can't measure up to the academy's standards, they may be required to leave the academy.

Cadets enjoy making waves when they take part in sports.

FACILITIES

The academy expects cadets to make athletics a part of their daily life. This is why it's no surprise that the academy is equipped with state-of-the-art athletic facilities. There are two swimming pools, four basketball courts, two gyms, baseball and softball fields, and a football stadium. The academy also has a fully-equipped rowing center and a seamanship sailing center.

EXTRACURRICULAR ACTIVITIES

Cadets are encouraged to participate in extracurricular activities. There are many clubs and activities to get involved in at the Coast Guard Academy. One of these clubs is the Windjammer Drum and Bugle Corps. This band tours all over the United States. There are also many volunteer opportunities in the local community surrounding the academy. Many cadets spend quality time with local kids by volunteering at the Big Brothers Big Sisters of America.

LIBERTY

Liberty is an authorized amount of time away from the academy. It's like having a day off. Liberty doesn't come easy at the academy. This is especially true in a fourth class cadet's first year. If fourth class

Strike up the band! Many cadets join the academy's marching band.

Everybody loves a parade at the Coast Guard Academy. Marching in the Color Guard is a time-honored tradition.

cadets pass inspection, which rarely happens the first time, they get liberty on Saturday afternoons. Sundays, all cadets have liberty all day. As cadets become upperclassmen, they get more and more liberty. Vacation time is also pretty limited, especially since cadets train through the summer.

TRADITION

The Coast Guard Academy is all about tradition. Some of these traditions are formal, such as attending formal dances and parades. Other traditions are informal. One informal tradition is Hundredth Day for fourth classmen. This is the day that fourth class gets to switch roles with second class. Fourth class cadets look forward to this day with much anticipation. What they don't realize is that the day before Hundredth Day, second class cadets make the swabs run around all night on silly errands. If the swabs don't return from the errands in time, they may be forced to do sit-ups and push-ups. By the time Hundredth Day comes along, fourth class cadets are so tired from the night before, that this payback day doesn't seem like too much fun.

Beyond the Academy

Cadets have a long road to graduation day. In that time they will have met many challenges and will have had many new experiences. When cadets finally reach the end of their last year at the academy, their adventures truly begin. Each cadet is commissioned as an ensign in the U.S. Coast Guard. These junior officers are usually assigned to duty as a deck watch officer or an engineering officer aboard a Coast Guard ship. It is standard to hold these positions for about two years. After that, officers specialize in other areas aboard the ship.

Cadets are assigned to locations based on how well they performed at the academy. New officers who graduated at the top of their class get the best assignments. This could include

Three cheers for the cadets! Having graduated the academy, the cadets look forward to a future where the sky's the limit!

being assigned to a ship off the coast of Alaska, Hawaii, or California. Whatever the assignment, the new ensign approaches it with pride and confidence.

LIFE AT SEA

Deck officers have many responsibilities. They may be assigned as the weapons officer. Weapons officers are in charge of maintaining the ship's deck cannons, small arms, and ammunition. These weapons need to be cleaned and kept in working condition at all times. Deck watch officers can also qualify as conning officers. A conning officer is responsible for navigating the ship, while managing several crewmen. One crewman mans the helm, or the wheel, another monitors the radar, and a third stands lookout. The conning officer is responsible for making sure everybody works as a team.

Eventually, an ensign may become a boarding officer. He or she takes charge of boarding parties when the Coast Guard needs to search another ship for illegal drugs or violations of fishing laws. This can be tricky business and the officer needs to know the laws well. The officer also needs to make sure that the boarding party under his or her command remains safe at all times.

Life at sea for a Coast Guard Academy graduate is fast paced and exciting.

Deck officers also may be responsible for conducting search-and-rescue operations. The officer in charge is responsible for making sure that calls for help from other ships are answered quickly and safely. All the training that these officers received at the Coast Guard Academy leaves them well prepared for their jobs.

AFTER THE SEA

Some Coast Guard Academy graduates remain in the Coast Guard for their entire careers. Others leave after their required five years are finished to take civilian jobs. Service in the Coast Guard gives young men and women a lot of technical experience. Many pursue careers in civil engineering. Others go on to careers that have nothing to do with engineering. Bruce Melnick was the first Coast Guard graduate to become an astronaut. Other gradutes become executives in corporate America. As Coast Guard officers, their experience making quick decisions, working well under pressure, and directing others prepared them for many different kinds of opportunities.

The Coast Guard Academy's strict military lifestyle requires a special kind of dedication and hard work. The decision to enter the Coast Guard Academy is one that should not be made lightly. It will change your life forever. In four years, you become a trained sailor, ready for active duty in the U.S Coast Guard. For the right person, attending the Coast Guard Academy can be a very rewarding experience.

The cadets fresh out of the academy are always ready to give a hand to people in trouble.

NEW WORDS

application a form that is used for acceptance to college

barque a sailing ship with three or more masts

boarding party Coast Guard officers and sailors who go aboard a ship that has been stopped for illegal activities

bugle a musical instrument shaped like a trumpet, but without keys

cadet a student at a military or naval academy

civilian having to do with someone who is not a member of the armed forces

cutter a single-masted ship

demerits marks against someone, usually for doing something wrong

extracurricular having to do with student activities that are outside of the regular school routine

NEW WORDS

honor respect earned from others

intercollegiate participating in activities with other colleges, usually in sports

intramural competing teams within one's own college

masts long poles that rise from the deck of a ship

navigation the science of getting ships from place to place

officer someone who is in charge of other people and is in a position of responsibility in the armed forces

requirements things that you need to do or have

reveille a piece of music used as a morning wake-up call

schooner a two-masted ship

FOR FURTHER READING

Gaines, Ann Graham. *The Coast Guard in Action*. Berkeley Heights, NJ: Enslow Publishers, 2001.

Green, Michael. *The U.S. Coast Guard*. Mankato, MN: Capstone Press, 2000.

Holden, Henry M. *Coast Guard Rescue and Patrol*. Berkeley Heights, NJ: Enslow Publishers, Incorporated, 2002.

Johnson, Robert Erwin. *Guardians of the Sea: History of the United States Coast Guard, 1915 to the Present*. Annapolis, MD: United States Naval Institute, 2000.

Krietemeyer, Captain George E. *The Coast Guardsman's Manual*. Annapolis, MD: United States Naval Institute, 2000.

Van Orden, M.D. *U.S. Navy Ships and Coast Guard Cutters*. Annapolis, MD: United States Naval Institute Press, 2000.

RESOURCES

Organization

THE UNITED STATES
COAST GUARD ACADEMY

Director of Admissions

U.S. Coast Guard Academy
31 Mohegan Avenue
New London, CT 06320-8103
(860) 444-8501

RESOURCES

Web Sites

THE UNITED STATES COAST GUARD ACADEMY'S OFFICIAL WEB SITE

www.cga.edu

This Web site has a lot of information about life in the Coast Guard Academy. Find out how to apply, what classes are offered, and what events are coming up.

THE UNITED STATES COAST GUARD'S OFFICIAL WEB SITE

www.uscg.mil/

This Web site has a lot of information on the Coast Guard. Find out the latest Coast Guard news, get information about different Coast Guard ships, and follow links to other Coast Guard related sites.

INDEX

INDEX

ABOUT THE AUTHOR

Aileen Weintraub is a freelance author and editor living in the scenic Hudson Valley in upstate New York. She has published over 30 young adult and children's books, edits historical manuscripts and college textbooks, and works part time for a not-for-profit organization serving children with special needs.